**Living L♥ve Forward**

What's Your Pet Peeve?

A Children's Leadership Series

Written by Kim Dawson
Illustrated by Paige Anocibar

Publisher: Tandem Services Press
PO Box 220, Yucaipa, CA 92399
www.tandemservicesink.com

Book Design by Paige Anocibar

ISBN 978-1-954986-27-5

Appreciation to

Inland Leaders Charter School and all our teachers and staff for inspiring and supporting me to write this series.

All my students and their families who taught me to be a better teacher and person.

The 3rd, 4th, and 5th grade classes at Inland Leaders who gave me GREAT feedback and helped me make this story better!

Logan for inspiring me to create a new character named Matthew. He is just as awesome as you are.

Pelican Elementary in Oregon for letting us use their school as a model for Lexie's Huckleberry Elementary.

My family and friends who have never wavered in supporting and encouraging my mission to help others.

Paige, my illustrator, for putting up with my "creative" tangents.

Jennifer Crosswhite, my editor and friend, who has been my sounding board and always keeps me positive when I hit the many bumps in the road. (https://www.tandemservicesink.com)

All my readers who have supported me and helped me spread the message that kids can be leaders too.

Sending a ton of love and encouragement to all of you!
We got this!

From the author of the series Living Love Forward:

I wrote this children's leadership series to create an open conversation about the experiences our kids face every day. Being a teacher for over two decades, I have created connections with kids of all ages. I have observed and learned a lot through these interactions and have discovered key skill sets that I think are important for their growth. My purpose in writing these sentimental and caring stories is the hope that they instill life skills and resilience in our children. In turn, this empowers them to become successful and compassionate people, as well as strong leaders. Join Lexie and our children as they navigate this journey of self-discovery.

Please note that this series can be used in conjunction with any Leadership Program focused on survival skills and effective habits for children.

This book specifically focuses on:

- **Frustration**
- **Anger**
- **Triggers**
- **Impulsivity**
- **Negative attitude**
- **Coping skills**
- **Upset**
- **Responsibility**
- **Accountability**
- **Self-awareness**
- **Problem and Solution**

Map of Harlow

Train Station

1st Street
1st Street
2nd Street
2nd Street
3r

Church Of Hope

Cemetery

Liberty Library

Rose Road

Daisy Lane

4th Street

Main Street

Lexie's House

Main Street

Bus Stop

6th St

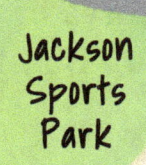

Main Street

Jackson Sports Park

Jasmine Avenue

Rose Road

Lavendar Lane

Lotus Loop

Riverside Park

Rose Road

Lavendar Lane

Huckleberry Elementary

Lavendar Lane

Annabelle's House

Jasmine Avenue

Jasmine Avenue

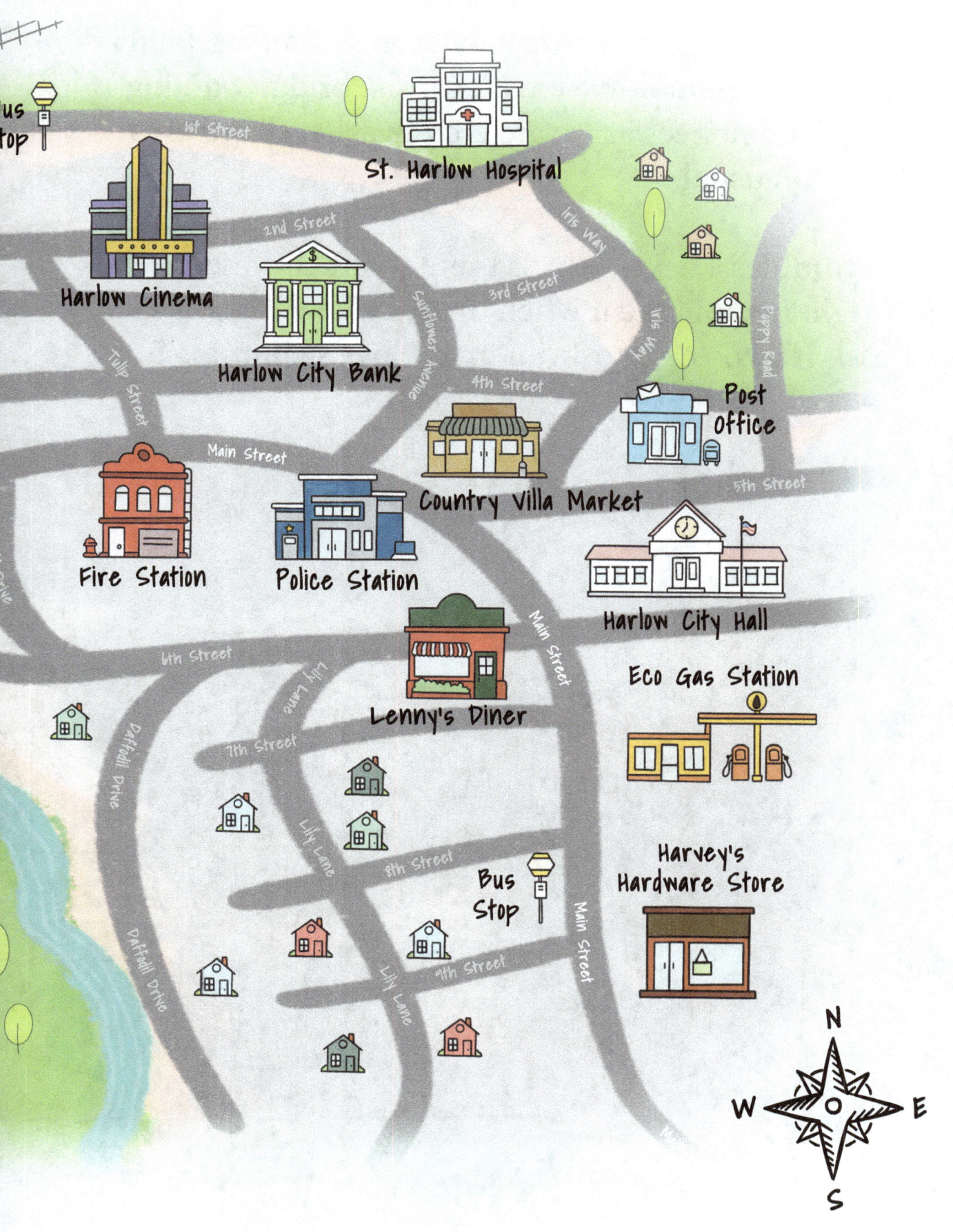

One sunny but cold morning, my brother Sam and I head out to walk to school. We cross over the bridge walking quickly. Sam notices as we are crossing that the river is higher than usual.

Sam grumbles, "Lexie, why is there so much water in the river right now? I hate it when the river is so high because it means it is too cold to swim in it! I love swimming."

"Dad would call that your pet peeve, Sam," I tease, "You remember, pet peeves are things that trigger us to get upset easily." Then, as I look over the railing to the water below, I continue, "You're right! I don't think I have ever seen it this full."

"I think it is the runoff from all the snow melting," Sam shares.

Nodding my head, I think about how we have had a lot of snowfall this winter and how nice it is to be able to go outside again. Breathing in the crisp air, we hurry our steps so we aren't late for school.

We arrive right when the bell is ringing. We hurry to our classrooms so we won't be late. I hang my coat up on the coat rack as I say hi to my best friend Annabelle.

We sit next to each other in class and try not to talk to each other too much. We aren't always good at it and sometimes we get in trouble. So far, Mrs. Bryce hasn't separated us, so we are going to keep trying not to talk so we don't get in trouble.

"Good morning, class," Mrs. Bryce says. We all call out good morning and we get right to work on our morning activities. After a while, she motions for us to go to the carpet area for reading time. Once we are all settled, she starts to read us this story about friendship. As she is reading, Charlie holds up his hand and asks about one of the words in the story. He says, "What does pet peeve mean, Mrs. Bryce?"

Mrs. Bryce goes back into the story where the word came up and rereads the sentence to us. Then she says, "A pet peeve is something that triggers you to get upset or angry when it happens. Generally, it is something that isn't a big deal, but it still upsets you. It can make you react in a way you wouldn't usually. Sometimes, we even take this frustration out on others and that isn't okay either. Everyone has different pet peeves. The trick is to figure out what yours are and find a solution so that when it happens it doesn't upset you." Listening to her, makes me think of the conversation Sam and I had this morning about the fullness of the river being his pet peeve.

Mrs Bryce shares one of her pet peeves. "I hate emptying the dishwasher. I don't mind cleaning the dishes or even stacking them in the dishwasher, but ask me to empty it after it is clean...sets me up every time. I get in a bad mood," She grins as she looks at us.

"You said we should find a solution to our pet peeves. What was yours?" Felix blurts out. He is always forgetting to raise his hand. Today, Mrs. Bryce doesn't seem to mind.

She calmly answers, "My husband and I discussed our pet peeves many years ago. He knows this one is mine, so he volunteered to be the official dishwasher emptier. He doesn't mind doing it, so it is easy for him to do that chore." She then asks us what our pet peeves are.

We all kind of look around or down at the floor. I don't think any of us have thought about it before. Mrs. Bryce notices and says that we can talk amongst ourselves and see if we can figure out what triggers us to get upset out of the blue. Everyone turns and starts talking to the person next to them.

After a few minutes, Mrs. Bryce calls for our attention and asks us again what our pet peeves are. Jackie raises her hand first and Mrs. Bryce calls on her.

"I hate pushing the grocery cart when we go to the Country Villa Market!" she shares. "Mom asked me once why I always get so grumpy when we go get groceries and I told her it was because I didn't like pushing the cart down the aisles. Laughingly, she said that it didn't bother her, so she would do it from now on. That was our solution and I was thankful that Mom had asked me."

Mrs. Bryce smiles at her and then asks if anyone else wants to share. I raise my hand and she calls on me.

"One of my chores at home is to empty the trash cans when they are full. I honestly don't mind doing this. What bugs me is putting a new bag in the trash can after I empty it. I don't know why I make a big deal about it. It isn't that hard, but it does make me grumpy as Jackie said. Dad and I talked about it once and he suggested that I leave the can without a bag in it. He would then put a bag in the trash can for me. It is working for us."

"That's my job at home too. I HATE taking out the trash! Lexie, can you come over and take out my trash for me?" Felix shouts out. We all laugh and start sharing our own stories.

Mrs. Bryce calms us all down again and asks for more volunteers to share. Matthew raises his hand and she points at him.

"My pet peeve is not being able to ride on the grass in my wheelchair. It is frustrating because I have to take the long way around when all the other kids can just cut through the grass. It is going to be expensive to get the kind of chair that can go off-roading, but I am saving my allowance and doing small jobs to try and buy a new one." Everyone smiles at him. If anyone deserves to go off-roading, it is Matthew. He never complains about anything and he always has a smile on his face. He is one of my friends too. Mrs. Bryce must agree too because she is nodding her head as she listens to Matthew.

"Anyone else?" she finally asks. Cindy raises her hand slightly as if unsure if she should share. "Go ahead, Cindy. What is your pet peeve?"

"Well...It is something that happens in class, so I don't know if I should share?" she says. Mrs. Bryce encourages her and she continues. "Well, It bothers me when people are chatty when they are suppose to be quiet." She pauses and looks around at the class. She continues by saying, "It is just really hard to concentrate when it happens and it frustrates me. Sometimes the whole class gets in trouble too when it is just a few kids. That isn't fair either." She leaves it there and looks at Mrs. Bryce.

Mrs. Bryce looks at her thoughtfully and says, "Actually, Cindy, it bugs me too. Maybe as a class, we can help come up with a solution for this pet peeve. Does anyone have any ideas?"

Felix calls out, "Maybe we can have a code word that we can shout out if it happens."

Mrs. Bryce looks at him in surprise. "That's an excellent idea," she says. "However, we won't shout it out. Maybe we quietly say it, so no one gets embarrassed. Now what should be the code word? Since it is your pet peeve, I think you should pick the word, Cindy."

I think you should pick the word, Cindy.

Cindy thinks a bit and then she says, "Purple monkeys."

The class agrees that if anyone hears purple monkeys quietly said in class then it means someone is having a hard time concentrating. We promise to all listen for the code word. We also promise to not get upset if we are the ones caught talking. We agree we want to try to help each other. Mrs. Bryce is always talking to us about being team players. This is a perfect example of that.

By the time we get done sharing our pet peeves, the bell rings and it is time for recess. I still can't stop thinking about Matthew's pet peeve though. We all had solutions to our pet peeves, but Matthew's seemed a lot harder to fix. A new wheelchair is expensive. After everyone leaves for recess, I approach Mrs. Bryce's desk to discuss this.

I tell her about my concerns and she listens. Then she says that she was thinking the same thing and was going to try and figure out a way to help. I nod and leave for recess, trusting that Mrs. Bryce will tell me when she figures something out.

Weeks go by before Mrs. Bryce pulls me aside to talk to me about Matthew's situation. I had almost forgotten about it...almost, but not totally. Matthew still smiles a lot, but I have seen that sad look when he sees the other kids cutting through the grass and knowing he can't. "Hey, Lexie," Mrs. Bryce says to me, "I talked to the principal about Matthew. He said he knew of an organization in town that helps in these kinds of situations and that he would reach out to them. We talked to Mathew's parents too and they are very appreciative of the thoughtfulness of everyone trying to help Matthew get a new wheelchair." I smile, excited for Matthew.

It's a Thursday morning. The bell rings and all the kids scatter to go line up for class. As I line up, I notice that Matthew isn't there. All of a sudden, I hear a "Look at me!!!" It's Mathew and he is racing to the line as he cuts across the grass with the other kids. He is in his new wheelchair. Everyone in line cheers and Matthew, with a big smile on his face, shows us his new chair.

Author's Advice

- Find out what your pet peeve is and what the solution is to fix it.

- If you get triggered really quickly about something, pause, take a breath, and see if it is a pet peeve that you didn't know about.

- Pet peeves are not excuses for being mean to others.

- Pet peeves are fixable, but you have to have a solution in order to fix them.

- If someone snaps at you, maybe it is a pet peeve. You should ask.

Think and Feel

What is your pet peeve? What is your solution to this problem? Share your answer with someone you trust.

Glossary

allowance

Definition: a sum of money given regularly or allowed for a particular purpose; giving money to children for doing weekly chores or jobs around the house

Part of Speech:

This word is a (noun, adjective, verb, adverb).

Evidence of how the word is used in the story.

Matthew is saving his allowance (money he gets from doing chores/jobs) to buy a new wheelchair.

appreciative

Definition: feeling of gratitude or thanks

Part of Speech:

This word is a (noun, adjective, verb, adverb).

Evidence of how the word is used in the story.

Matthew's parents were appreciative (feeling thankful) of the thoughtfulness of everyone trying to help their son.

Glossary

dishwasher

Definition: a machine that washes dishes, glasses, and pans

Part of Speech:

This word is a (**noun**, adjective, verb, adverb).

Evidence of how the word is used in the story.

Mrs. Bryce's pet peeve is emptying the dishwasher after the dishes are clean.

grumpy

Definition: in a bad mood; cranky; moody; irritable

Part of Speech:

This word is a (noun, **adjective**, verb, adverb).

Evidence of how the word is used in the story.

Jackie gets grumpy (cranky) when she has to push the shopping cart in the grocery store. Lexie is grumpy (irritable) if she has to put a new trash bag in the trashcan.

Glossary

out of the blue

Definition: without warning; unexpected

Part of Speech:

"out of the blue" is an idiom
(An idiom is a phrase that means something different than the literal words being used. Examples: "It is raining cats and dogs" means it is raining very hard and "Go break a leg!" means go try your hardest)

Evidence of how the word is used in the story.

Pet peeves can cause someone to get upset out of the blue (without warning or unexpectedly).

pet peeve

Definition: a cause of frustration, irritation, or annoyance; to be annoyed without warning

Language Usage:

This word is a (noun, adjective, verb, adverb).

Evidence of how the word is used in the story.

Matthew's pet peeve (frustration) is not being able to go through the grass in his wheelchair.

Glossary

scatter

Definition: to cause to separate or move in all different directions

Part of Speech:

This word is a (noun, adjective, verb, adverb).

Evidence of how the word is used in the story.

When the bell rings, the kids scatter (move in different directions) and race to line up for class.

team players

Definition: a group that works together to solve something; a team member who works for the good of the team, perhaps sacrificing his or her interests or goals.

Part of Speech:

This word is a (noun, adjective, verb, adverb).

Evidence of how the word is used in the story.

Everyone is a team player (works together) when they try to find a solution to Cindy's pet peeve of people tapping pencils on the desk.

Glossary

trigger

Definition: to cause, or set off a behavior

Part of Speech:

This word is a (noun, adjective, verb, adverb).

Evidence of how the word is used in the story.

Everyone's pet peeves triggers (cause) frustration when they happen.

wheelchair

Definition: a chair on two large wheels that is used by people who cannot walk from place to place.

Part of Speech:

This word is a (noun, adjective, verb, adverb).

Evidence of how the word is used in the story.

Matthew is in a wheelchair because he can not walk on his own.

About the Author: Kim Dawson

I am a single mom of two wonderful kids. I have been teaching for a number of decades and love spending time with my students. I have been writing since I was a child. It has always been a way for me to express myself when I am struggling. I strongly believe that we do not give our kids the credit they deserve. They have a lot to teach us if we just listen.

About the Illustrator: Paige Anocibar

Art is my passion. Every day I am thankful to have a career that empowers me to express myself through creativity. Drawing has been a part of my life since I was a small child. Coloring and painting were my favorite part of going to school. Back then, just like now, I was eager for the next art project. I knew that expressing myself through art is all I have ever wanted to do with my life, and illustrating this book has helped me achieve a part of that dream.

If you enjoyed this story, see other books in this Children's Leadership series, Living Love Forward.

2023 Books

February   May   September   November

2024 Books

March   May   September   November